Glencoe
Literature
The Reader's Choice

Fluency Practice
and Assessment

Mc Graw Hill Glencoe

New York, New York   Columbus, Ohio   Chicago, Illinois   Woodland Hills, California

Acknowledgments

Excerpt from "The Talking Skull" from *A Pride of African Tales* by Donna Washington, illustrated by James Ransome. Text copyright © 2004 by Donna Washington. Used by permission of HarperCollins Publishers.

Excerpt from "The Circuit" by Francisco Jiminez. Reprinted by permission of the author.

Excerpt from "Charles" from *The Lottery* by Shirley Jackson. Copyright © 1948, 1949 by Shirley Jackson, and copyright renewed © 1976 by Laurence Hyman, Barry Hyman, Mrs. Sarah Webster, and Mrs. Joanne Schnurer.

Excerpt from "Priscilla and the Wimps" by Richard Peck, from *Sixteen: Short Stories* ed. by Donald R. Gallo. Copyright © 1995 by Scholastic, Inc.

Excerpt from *Rosa Parks: My Story* by Rosa Parks with Jim Haskins. Copyright © 1992 by Rosa Parks.

Excerpt from "Aunt Millicent" by Mary Steele, from *Dream Time*, edited by Toss Gascoigne, Jo Goodman, and Margot Tyrell. Copyright © 1989 by Mary Steele. Collection copyright © 1989 by the Children's Book Council of Australia. Reprinted by permission of Houghton Mifflin Co. All rights reserved.

Excerpt from "What Makes Teens Tick?" by Claudia Wallis, updated 2005 © Time Inc.

Excerpt from *Harriet Tubman: Conductor of the Underground Railroad* by Ann Petry. Reprinted by permission of Russel & Volkening as agents for the author. Copyright © 1955 by Ann Petry, renewed in 1983 by Ann Petry.

Excerpt from "The Monsters Are Due on Maple Street" by Rod Serling. All rights reserved. © 1960 Rod Serling; © 1988 by Carolyn Serling, Jodi Serling, and Anne Serling.

Excerpt from "I Have a Dream" reprinted by arrangement with the Estate of Martin Luther King Jr., c/o Writers House as agent for the proprietor New York, NY. Copyright 1963 Martin Luther King Jr., copyright renewed 1991 by Coretta Scott King.

Excerpt from *A Child's Christmas in Wales* by Dylan Thomas. Copyright © 1954 by New Directions Publishing Corp. Reprinted by permission of New Directions Publishing Corp.

The McGraw-Hill Companies

Send all inquiries to:
Glencoe/McGraw-Hill
8787 Orion Place
Columbus, OH 43240-4027

10-digit ISBN 0-07-876840-3
13-digit ISBN 978-0-07-876840-8

Printed in the United States of America.
3 4 5 6 7 8   054   10 09 08 07

Table of Contents

To the Teacher

Practice, Practice, Practice

Fluency (the rate and accuracy with which students read) is highly correlated with comprehension and is one of the best indicators of overall reading ability. **Initial Screening and Fluency Assessment** provides two ways to look at oral reading fluency.

- **Initial Screening Assessment** The purpose of this assessment is to determine whether a student has the reading proficiency to work successfully in *Glencoe Literature: Reading with Purpose* or whether he or she would benefit from strategic intervention or the literacy intervention curriculum Jamestown *Reading Fluency* program. The screening assessment provides you with a set of seven oral reading sentences. By noting the errors a student makes when reading the sentences aloud, you receive immediate insight into the student's general reading ability so you can appropriately match the student with the instructional materials that will foster growth as a strategic and engaged reader.

- **Fluency Assessment** These timed, one-minute fluency passages provide an efficient and accurate way to track reading behaviors. The passages give you an easy and straightforward way to monitor reading growth throughout the school year. In the same way that a class photo captures a student at a certain time and place, a fluency "photo" captures a student's reading behaviors at one given point and allows you to document how reading skills develop over time.

Establishing the Home Connection Family members are powerful allies for teachers; they can provide invaluable help in building students' reading skills and interests outside the classroom. By clearly communicating fluency assessment scores to parents and guardians, you can assure family members of their student's reading progress. The more a student practices reading aloud from familiar, enjoyable texts, the more fluency and confidence the student develops. By sending home stories and other selected texts for students to read aloud with their families, you not only help develop the student's fluency but also help build strong connections between students, family, teachers, and texts.

Using Oral Fluency Assessments

The purpose of assessment is to inform instruction. Choosing the best instructional materials and teaching strategies for each student depends on accurately assessing a student's skills. To enable students to demonstrate their true abilities, help them feel comfortable and confident as they read for you. The following guidelines will help you administer the oral fluency assessments included in this book.

- Each assessment in this booklet includes a reading passage for students and a corresponding teacher scoring page on which you can record individual results. The scoring page is printed on the back of the reading passage. For each fluency survey, you will need only one copy of the reading passage (because the reading passage will be used by all the students, you may wish to laminate it); however, you will need to make a copy of the scoring page for each student you will assess. Do **not** let students read from a teacher scoring page—the scoring guide and the added information for the teacher can make students feel anxious and thus diminish the effectiveness of the assessments.

- Be sure to use the same passage for all students during one fluency survey.

- Assess each student individually in a quiet place with few distractions. Each assessment should take only a few minutes. If you assess a few of the students each day, you can survey your entire class over a period of several days without interrupting the flow of your normal classroom activities.

- Have the student sit across from you so that he or she is not distracted from reading by what you are writing. Begin by explaining the process. Tell the student that you want him or her to read the sentences or the passage at a comfortable rate and as accurately as possible. You may wish to explain that students who concentrate only on reading fast may stumble unnecessarily. Answer any questions the student may have but do not allow him or her to preview the selection. Place a blank sheet of paper over the reading passage until the student is ready to begin reading.

- See specific assessment directions for how to score errors. When a student reads a word incorrectly, make a mark through that word in the text on the scoring page. You may wish to use a simple slash mark each time the student makes an error, or you may use the specific marks from the chart on the next page. Allow the student to complete the sentences or passage regardless of the number of errors he or she

Administering the Initial Screening

The purpose of this assessment is to determine whether a student has sufficient reading proficiency to work successfully in *Glencoe Literature: Reading with Purpose*. The assessment tool is a set of seven oral reading sentences. By asking students to read sentences aloud, you can get a quick measure of each student's reading ability.

Use these guidelines to help you administer and score the Initial Screening Assessment.

- Read and follow the general directions on page 1 of this book for administering oral fluency assessments.

- As each student reads the sentences aloud, mark the scoring page by underlining or drawing a mark through words the student reads incorrectly.

> For the Initial Screening Assessment, do not score as errors the misreading of small words such as *to*, *they*, or *of*. Do not score as errors inserted words or omissions of word endings.

- The scoring rubric below will assist you in determining whether a student can work successfully with *Glencoe Literature: Reading with Purpose*.

0-2 errors The student can independently read the selections in *Glencoe Literature: Reading with Purpose*.

3-4 errors The student will require some guided reading instruction and may benefit from strategic intervention to successfully use *Glencoe Literature: Reading with Purpose*.

5+ errors The student will most likely need the Jamestown *Reading Fluency* program.

Student Page—Reading Sentences

1. It's much less for me to do.
2. Sometimes we joined our aunts and uncles and drove in a caravan out to the park or to the beach.
3. From the distant mountains came a terrible roar.
4. He now hurried forth, and hastened to his old resort, the village inn— but it too was gone.
5. When the first sunlight fell through the roof, he raised one eyelid cautiously.
6. The whole neighborhood abounds with local tales, haunted spots, and twilight superstitions.
7. I have to take care of my brother until my mom comes home from work.

Scoring Page–Initial Screening Assessment

Directions: Mark this copy of the sentences by underlining or drawing a line through each reading error the student makes. Do **not** score as errors the misreading of small words such as *to*, *they*, or *of*. Do **not** score as errors inserted words or omissions of word endings. Use the box below the sentences to record the student's score (number of errors) along with any other notes that might be helpful.

1. It's much less for me to do.

2. Sometimes we joined our aunts and uncles and drove in a caravan out to the park or to the beach.

3. From the distant mountains came a terrible roar.

4. He now hurried forth, and hastened to his old resort, the village inn—but it too was gone.

5. When the first sunlight fell through the roof, he raised one eyelid cautiously.

6. The whole neighborhood abounds with local tales, haunted spots, and twilight superstitions.

7. I have to take care of my brother until my mom comes home from work.

Teacher's comments

_____

_____

- The scoring rubric below will assist you in determining whether a student can work successfully with *Glencoe Literature: Reading with Purpose*.

0-2 errors reads with ease	**Student's Score** _____	
3-4 errors reads with help	**Comments** _____	
5+ errors needs intervention	_____	
	_____	

Fluency Assessment

Administering the Fluency Assessments

A timed, one-minute fluency assessment is a quick way to monitor the reading progress of your students. The fluency passages that follow are passages taken from *Glencoe Literature: Reading with Purpose*. The passages are marked with a Lexile readability value. The passages, which are approximately 150-200 words long, gradually progress in difficulty. The following guidelines will help you administer the fluency assessment.

- Read and follow the general directions for using oral fluency assessments found on page 1 of this book.

- Each fluency assessment includes a teacher scoring page (with word counts marked and with space to write comments and to record results) and a reading passage for students. The reading passage is on the back of the scoring page. You will need only one copy of the reading passage; however, you will need to make a copy of the scoring guide for each student you assess. Do not let students read from a scoring page—the scoring guide and the added information for the teacher can make students feel anxious and thus diminish the effectiveness of the assessments.

- You may wish to use the **Student Fluency Progress Chart** on page 7 to keep progress charts for individual students.

- Tell the student that you want him or her to read the passage at a comfortable rate and as accurately as possible. Explain that you will time the oral reading for one minute and will tell him or her when to begin reading. Do not allow students to preview the selections.

- Tell students when to begin. Start the one-minute timing with the first line of text. When a student makes a reading error, draw a mark through that word on the scoring page. **For these assessments count all errors the student makes.** At the end of one minute, make a slash mark to indicate the last word the student reads but allow him or her to complete the passage uninterrupted.

- To arrive at the correct words-per-minute score, count the number of words read in one minute and subtract the total errors made in that time.

- You may wish to record additional information on the scoring pages, such as words that a student uses as substitutions or places where a student repeats words. You might also make a general comment—for example, "student stumbles on multisyllabic words," or "student reads expressively."

Marking Reading Errors

As you score the assessments in this book, you may wish to use these specific marks to indicate the following types of reading errors.

Type of Reading Error	How to Mark It
Substitutions (words misread or mispronounced)	**Draw a line through the word.** The boy felt ~~confused~~.
Omissions (words skipped)	**Circle the word the student skips.** He went to (see) Grandpa.
Insertions (words added that are not in the text)	**Draw a ∧ where the student adds a word.** She climbed ∧over the fence.
Word reversals	**Use a ∪ to show word reversal.** They were truly excited.
Self-corrections (words student spontaneously corrects)	**Draw a line through the misread word. Write *sc* above self-corrected error.** The family bought a new ~~house~~. *sc*
Examiner's help	**Write an H above the word where you have helped a student.** Do **not** offer help unless a student has struggled for approximately ten seconds.
Recurring errors	**Count a recurring error—such as mispronouncing a proper noun or repeatedly stumbling on the same difficult word—as one error.**

Fluency Practice and Assessment

Student Fluency Progress Chart

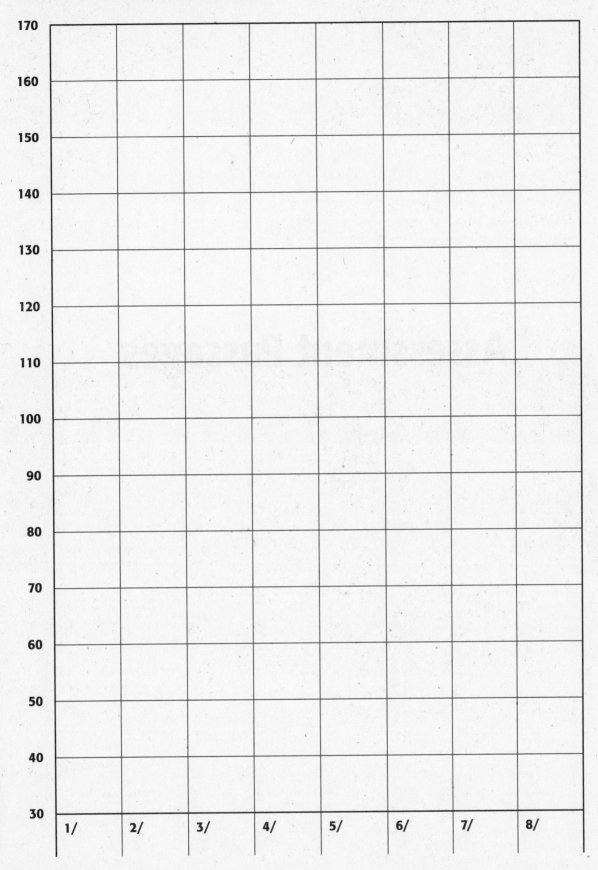

Name _____

Assessment Passages

from **The Talking Skull**

by Donna L. Washington

Once a man was walking down the road toward his village. He was not paying attention to anything around him. This man considered himself a scholar of life. He was always deep in thought. He liked to think about important things. He did not put his mind to ordinary problems. If it wasn't impossible, or at least very complicated, he didn't care about it at all.

This man spent all day looking out over the ocean, and he only noticed things he thought were useful. He didn't notice the beauty of the ocean. The only things he considered were sharks and shipwrecks. He didn't notice the clear blue sky. He was thinking about all the storms that must have been churning far away. He did not notice the wonderful songs of the birds. He only thought about how many of their nests had been robbed. He didn't notice the playful animals swinging through the branches or rustling in the grass. He only wondered whether or not the great cats were on the prowl. That was the kind of man he was.

from **The Talking Skull**

by Donna L. Washington

Once a man was walking down the road	8
toward his village. He was not paying attention	16
to anything around him. This man considered	23
himself a scholar of life. He was always deep	32
in thought. He liked to think about important	40
things. He did not put his mind to ordinary	49
problems. If it wasn't impossible, or at least	57
very complicated, he didn't care about it at all.	66
This man spent all day looking out over the	75
ocean, and he only noticed things he thought	83
were useful. He didn't notice the beauty of	91
the ocean. The only things he considered	98
were sharks and shipwrecks. He didn't notice	105
the clear blue sky. He was thinking about all	114
the storms that must have been churning far	122
away. He did not notice the wonderful songs	130
of the birds. He only thought about how many	139
of their nests had been robbed. He didn't	147
notice the playful animals swinging through	153
the branches or rustling in the grass. He only	162
wondered whether or not the great cats were on	171
the prowl. That was the kind of man he was.	181

0-2 errors reads with ease	**Student's Score** _____	
3-4 errors reads with help	**Comments**_____	
5+ errors needs intervention	_____	
	_____	

from **The Circuit**

by Francisco Jimenez

As we drove home Papa did not say a word. With both hands on the wheel, he stared at the dirt road. My older brother, Roberto, was also silent. He leaned his head back and closed his eyes. Once in a while he cleared from his throat the dust that blew in from outside.

Yes, it was that time of year. When I opened the front door to the shack, I stopped. Everything we owned was neatly packed in cardboard boxes. Suddenly I felt even more the weight of hours, days, weeks, and months of work. I sat down on a box. The thought of having to move to Fresno and knowing what was in store for me there brought tears to my eyes.

That night I could not sleep. I lay in bed thinking about how much I hated this move.

A little before five o'clock in the morning, Papa woke everyone up.

from **The Circuit**

by Francisco Jimenez

As we drove home Papa did not say a	9
word. With both hands on the wheel, he	17
stared at the dirt road. My older brother,	25
Roberto, was also silent. He leaned his	32
head back and closed his eyes. Once in a	41
while he cleared from his throat the dust	49
that blew in from outside.	54
Yes, it was that time of year. When I	63
opened the front door to the shack, I	71
stopped. Everything we owned was neatly	77
packed in cardboard boxes. Suddenly I felt	84
even more the weight of hours, days,	91
weeks, and months of work. I sat down on	100
a box. The thought of having to move to	109
Fresno and knowing what was in store for	117
me there brought tears to my eyes.	124
That night I could not sleep. I lay in	133
bed thinking about how much I hated this	141
move.	142
A little before five o'clock in the	149
morning, Papa woke everyone up.	154

0-2 errors	reads with ease	**Student's Score** _____
3-4 errors	reads with help	**Comments** _____
5+ errors	needs intervention	_____
		_____

from **Charles**

by Shirley Jackson

The day my son Laurie started kindergarten he renounced corduroy overalls with bibs and began wearing blue jeans with a belt; I watched him go off the first morning with the older girl next door, seeing clearly that an era of my life was ended, my sweet-voiced nursery-school tot replaced by a long-trousered, swaggering character who forgot to stop at the corner and wave good-bye to me.

He came home the same way, the front door slamming open, his cap on the floor, and the voice suddenly become raucous shouting, "Isn't anybody *here*?"

At lunch he spoke insolently to his father, spilled his baby sister's milk, and remarked that his teacher said we were not to take the name of the Lord in vain.

"How was school today?" I asked, elaborately casual.

"All right," he said

"Did you learn anything?" his father asked.

Laurie regarded his father coldly. "I didn't learn nothing," he said.

from **Charles**

by Shirley Jackson

The day my son Laurie started kindergarten	7
he renounced corduroy overalls with bibs	13
and began wearing blue jeans with a belt; I	21
watched him go off the first morning with	30
the older girl next door, seeing clearly that an	39
era of my life was ended, my sweet-voiced	47
nursery-school tot replaced by a	52
long-trousered, swaggering character who	56
forgot to stop at the corner and wave	64
good-bye to me.	67
He came home the same way, the front	75
door slamming open, his cap on the floor,	83
and the voice suddenly become raucous	89
shouting, "Isn't anybody *here*?"	93
At lunch he spoke insolently to his	100
father, spilled his baby sister's milk, and	107
remarked that his teacher said we were not	115
to take the name of the Lord in vain.	124
"How was school today?" I asked,	130
elaborately casual.	132
"All right," he said	136
"Did you learn anything?" his father	142
asked.	143
Laurie regarded his father coldly. "I	149
didn't learn nothing," he said.	154

0-2 errors reads with ease	**Student's Score** _____
3-4 errors reads with help	**Comments**_____
5+ errors needs intervention	_____
	_____

from **Priscilla and the Wimps**

by Richard Peck

Listen, there was a time when you couldn't even go to the *rest room* around this school without a pass. And I'm not talking about those little pink tickets made out by some teacher. I'm talking about a pass that could cost anywhere up to a buck, sold by Monk Klutter.

Not that Mighty Monk ever touched money, not in public. The gang he ran, which ran the school for him, was his collection agency. They were Klutter's Kobras, spelled out in nailheads on six well-known black plastic windbreakers.

Monk's threads were more . . . subtle. A pile-lined suede battle jacket with lizard-skin flaps over tailored Levis and a pair of ostrich-skin boots, brassed-toed and suitable for kicking people around. One of his Kobras did nothing all day but walk a half step behind Monk, carrying a fitted bag with Monk's gym shoes, a roll of restroom passes, a cashbox, and a switchblade that Monk gave himself manicures with at lunch over at the Kobra's table.

from **Priscilla and the Wimps"**

by Richard Peck

Listen, there was a time when you	7
couldn't even go to the *rest room* around	15
this school without a pass. And I'm not	23
talking about those little pink tickets made	30
out by some teacher. I'm talking about a	38
pass that could cost anywhere up to a buck,	47
sold by Monk Klutter.	51
Not that Mighty Monk ever touched	57
money, not in public. The gang he ran,	65
which ran the school for him, was his	73
collection agency. They were Klutter's	78
Kobras, spelled out in nailheads on	84
six well-known black plastic windbreakers.	89
Monk's threads were more . . . subtle.	94
A pile-lined suede battle jacket with	100
lizard-skin flaps over tailored Levis and a	107
pair of ostrich-skin boots, brassed-toed and	113
suitable for kicking people around. One of	120
his Kobras did nothing all day but walk a	129
half step behind Monk, carrying a fitted bag	137
with Monk's gym shoes, a roll of restroom	145
passes, a cashbox, and a switchblade that	152
Monk gave himself manicures with at lunch	159
over at the Kobra's table.	164

0-2 errors	reads with ease	**Student's Score** _____
3-4 errors	reads with help	**Comments**_____
5+ errors	needs intervention	_____
		_____

from **Rosa Parks: My Story**

by Rosa Parks with Jim Haskins

The driver saw me still sitting there, and he asked was I going to stand up. I said, "No." He said, "Well, I'm going to have you arrested." Then I said, "You may do that." These were the only words we said to each other. I didn't even know his name, which was James Blake, until we were in court together. He got out of the bus and stayed outside for a few minutes, waiting for the police.

As I sat there, I tried not to think about what might happen. I knew that anything was possible. I could be manhandled or beaten. I could be arrested. People have asked me if it occurred to me then that I could be the test case the NAACP had been looking for. I did not think about that at all. In fact if I had let myself think too deeply about what might happen to me, I might have gotten off the bus. But I chose to remain.

from **Rosa Parks: My Story**

by Rosa Parks with Jim Haskins

The driver saw me still sitting there,	7
and he asked was I going to stand up.	16
I said, "No." He said, "Well, I'm going to	25
have you arrested." Then I said, "You may	33
do that." These were the only words we	41
said to each other. I didn't even know his	50
name, which was James Blake, until we	57
were in court together. He got out of the	66
bus and stayed outside for a few minutes,	74
waiting for the police.	78
As I sat there, I tried not to think about	88
what might happen. I knew that anything	95
was possible. I could be manhandled or	102
beaten. I could be arrested. People have	109
asked me if it occurred to me then that I	119
could be the test case the NAACP had been	128
looking for. I did not think about that at all.	138
In fact if I had let myself think too deeply	148
about what might happen to me, I might	156
have gotten off the bus. But I chose to remain.	166

0-2 errors	reads with ease	**Student's Score** _____
3-4 errors	reads with help	**Comments**_____
5+ errors	needs intervention	_____
		_____

from **Aunt Millicent**

by Mary Steele

Grandma pondered a moment. "Now that you mention it, she did. She did indeed. I thought we'd have to chain her up sometime! We lived near the edge of town, you'll remember, and Millie would look out towards the paddocks and hills and say that she wanted to know what was over the horizon, or where the birds were flying to, or where the clouds came from behind the hills. We never knew where she'd be off to next—but she certainly ended up in the right job! I'm so glad she became an explorer. If I were a bit younger and had better feet, I might even go and join her. It would be most interesting to see the Cameroons. It's full of monkeys, I believe."

"Was Aunt Millicent good at geography at school?" Nerissa remembered to ask.

"Let me think—yes, she must have been because one year she won a prize for it, and the prize was a book called *Lives of the Great Explorers*."

from **Aunt Millicent**

by Mary Steele

Grandma pondered a moment. "Now	5
that you mention it, she did. She did indeed.	14
I thought we'd have to chain her up sometime!	23
We lived near the edge of town, you'll	31
remember, and Millie would look out towards	38
the paddocks and hills and say that she wanted	47
to know what was over the horizon, or where	56
the birds were flying to, or where the clouds	65
came from behind the hills. We never knew	73
where she'd be off to next—but she certainly	82
ended up in the right job! I'm so glad she	92
became an explorer. If I were a bit younger	101
and had better feet, I might even go and join	111
her. It would be most interesting to see the	120
Cameroons. It's full of monkeys, I believe."	127
"Was Aunt Millicent good at geography at	134
school?" Nerissa remembered to ask.	139
"Let me think—yes, she must have been	147
because one year she won a prize for it, and	157
the prize was a book called *Lives of the Great*	167
Explorers."	168

0-2 errors reads with ease	**Student's Score** _____
3-4 errors reads with help	**Comments**_____
5+ errors needs intervention	_____
	_____

from **The Real Magic of Harry Potter**

by Nancy Gibbs

It's probably no surprise to Rowling's fans that many children buy the books with their own money. Or that they wear out flashlight batteries reading the books after lights-out. And, no surprise here, even readers who dislike thick books have read Harry Potter not once or twice but a dozen times. For many fans, the books are far better than watching TV or staring at a computer screen.

When the fifth book in the series, *Harry Potter and the Order of the Phoenix*, was published in June 2003, it created a lot of excitement. There were Potter parties complete with owls, cloaks, and butterbeer. Kids wore their Potter pajamas. They even wanted to sleep in a "cupboard under the stairs," as Harry is forced to do by his creepy adopted family on Privet Drive. Some families ordered two or three books so that everyone could read the book at the same time. At close to 900 pages, *Harry Potter and the Order of the Phoenix* is the longest children's book there is. It was the best seller online only two hours after it was possible for computer users to order copies of it.

from **The Real Magic of Harry Potter**

by Nancy Gibbs

It's probably no surprise to Rowling's fans 7
that many children buy the books with their 15
own money. Or that they wear out flashlight 23
batteries reading the books after lights-out. 29
And, no surprise here, even readers who dislike 37
thick books have read Harry Potter not once 45
or twice but a dozen times. For many fans, the 55
books are far better than watching TV or staring 64
at a computer screen. 68

When the fifth book in the series, *Harry* 76
Potter and the Order of the Phoenix, was 84
published in June 2003, it created a lot of 93
excitement. There were Potter parties complete 99
with owls, cloaks, and butterbeer. Kids wore 106
their Potter pajamas. They even wanted to sleep 114
in a "cupboard under the stairs," as Harry is 123
forced to do by his creepy adopted family on 132
Privet Drive. Some families ordered two or 139
three books so that everyone could read the 147
book at the same time. At close to 900 pages, 157
Harry Potter and the Order of the Phoenix is 166
the longest children's book there is. It was 174
the best seller online only two hours after it was 184
possible for computer users to order copies of it. 193

0-2 errors	reads with ease	**Student's Score** _____
3-4 errors	reads with help	**Comments**_____
5+ errors	needs intervention	_____
		_____

from **What Makes Teens Tick?**

by Claudia Wallis

Before birth, nerve cells in the brain undergo a phase in which they multiply and grow rapidly. Then the brain gets rid of cells that aren't needed. Giedd's studies show that brain cells undergo a second phase of change that starts in childhood and lasts until the early twenties. Unlike the earlier phase, which changes the number of nerve cells, the second one changes the number of connections between the nerve cells.

When a child is between 6 and 12 years old, nerve cells become bushier. Each nerve cell branches out to other nerve cells. These branches carry signals between the cells. This process peaks when girls are about 11 and boys are about $12\frac{1}{2}$ Then some of the branches are slowly thinned out over several years.

At the same time, a fatty layer covers the branches of the nerve cells that remain. With each passing year, the fatty coverings thicken, much like tree rings. During this time, a person's brain has fewer fast connections. It's a trade-off. The brain becomes more efficient but is probably losing its potential for learning and its ability to recover from trauma.

from **What Makes Teens Tick?**

by Claudia Wallis

Before birth, nerve cells in the brain	7
undergo a phase in which they multiply and	14
grow rapidly. Then the brain gets rid of cells	23
that aren't needed. Giedd's studies show that	30
brain cells undergo a second phase of change	38
that starts in childhood and lasts until the	46
early twenties. Unlike the earlier phase, which	53
changes the number of nerve cells, the second	61
one changes the number of connections between	68
the nerve cells.	71
When a child is between 6 and 12 years	80
old, nerve cells become bushier. Each nerve	87
cell branches out to other nerve cells. These	95
branches carry signals between the cells. This	102
process peaks when girls are about 11 and boys	111
are about $12\frac{1}{2}$ Then some of the branches are	121
slowly thinned out over several years.	127
At the same time, a fatty layer covers the	136
branches of the nerve cells that remain. With	144
each passing year, the fatty coverings thicken,	151
much like tree rings. During this time, a	159
person's brain has fewer fast connections. It's a	167
trade-off. The brain becomes more efficient but	174
is probably losing its potential for learning and	182
its ability to recover from trauma.	188

0-2 errors	reads with ease	**Student's Score** _____
3-4 errors	reads with help	**Comments**_____
5+ errors	needs intervention	_____
		_____

from Harriet Tubman: Conductor on the Underground Railroad

by Ann Petry

Harriet Tubman could have told them that there was more involved in this matter of running off slaves than signaling the would-be runaways by imitating the call of a whippoorwill, or a hoot owl, far more involved than a matter of waiting for a clear night when the North Star was visible.

In December, 1851, when she started out with the band of fugitives that she planned to take to Canada, she had been in the vicinity of the plantation for days, planning the trip, carefully selecting the slaves that she would take with her. She had announced her arrival in the quarter by singing the forbidden spiritual—"Go Down, Moses, 'way down to Egypt Land"—singing it softly outside the door of a slave cabin, late at night. The husky voice was beautiful even when it was barely more than a murmur borne on the wind.

Once she made her presence known, word of her coming spread from cabin to cabin. The slaves whispered to each other, ear to mouth, mouth to ear, "Moses is here." "Moses has come." "Get ready. Moses is back again."

from **Harriet Tubman: Conductor on the Underground Railroad**

by Ann Petry

Harriet Tubman could have told them that there	8
was more involved in this matter of running off	17
slaves than signaling the would-be runaways by	24
imitating the call of a whippoorwill, or a hoot owl,	34
far more involved than a matter of waiting for a	44
clear night when the North Star was visible.	52
In December, 1851, when she started out with	60
the band of fugitives that she planned to take to	70
Canada, she had been in the vicinity of the	79
plantation for days, planning the trip, carefully	86
selecting the slaves that she would take with her.	95
She had announced her arrival in the quarter by	104
singing the forbidden spiritual—"Go Down, Moses,	111
'way down to Egypt Land"—singing it softly	119
outside the door of a slave cabin, late at night. The	130
husky voice was beautiful even when it was barely	139
more than a murmur borne on the wind.	147
Once she made her presence known, word of her	156
coming spread from cabin to cabin. The slaves	164
whispered to each other, ear to mouth, mouth to ear,	174
"Moses is here." "Moses has come." "Get ready.	182
Moses is back again."	186

0-2 errors	reads with ease	**Student's Score** _____
3-4 errors	reads with help	**Comments**_____
5+ errors	needs intervention	_____
		_____

Reading with Expression

Practice Makes Perfect

Reading fluency is always important—no matter the age or grade, no matter a struggling reader or above-average reader. Fluency in reading allows every reader the luxury of leaving decoding behind and focusing on *what* is being read. Such fluency requires practice.

Reading fluency is not about teaching reading comprehension skills and strategies. It's not about test-taking skills; it's about *practice*. And more practice. The following passages, along with those connected to assessment, are designed to give your students practice in reading aloud from various genres, with a range of emotion, alone or in pairs or groups, and for different amounts of time.

The Value of Longer Passages

The following passages are longer and call for more mastery in fluency than do those passages used only for assessment. The longer passages help students develop this mastery, or *automaticity*, in which fluent readers read with no noticeable mental effort. They read with the ability to translate letters and sounds into words in an automatic way. This process requires no conscious thought. It is like playing a musical instrument or volleying in a tennis game.

Comprehension does require conscious thought. Word identification, however, can become automatic, without conscious effort. Fluency requires decoding words correctly. With longer selections especially, the rate, or speed is important. Slow reading can skew the text and weaken comprehension.

Reading with Expression

When you ask your students to read with expression, you expect their reading to reflect the meaning of what they are reading. Students show this expression by the variations in pitch, stress patterns, and duration they use. In other words, they read as if they were speaking.

To help students develop fluency in reading, note whether:

✓ they show by inflection an understanding of punctuation—for example, their voice should rise at the end of a question or reflect urgency when they see an exclamation point;

✓ their vocal tone appropriately reflects the character's mental or emotional state—for example, the student's voice should show excitement, fear, or confidence in a character;

✓ punctuation—such as phrases or conjunctions—prompts the reader to pause.

The passages that follow give students a variety of ways to place emphases on the right words, to use inflection and intonation appropriately, to display a character's feeling, and to understand how the punctuation influences phrasing.

Suggested Ways for Building Fluency

Here are some methods to use with your students for building fluency:

• **model** fluent oral reading by reading aloud the passages;

• provide support with **choral** and **echo reading**, **paired reading**, and **tape-recorded reading**

• suggest passages suitable for **Readers Theater** and/or **Radio Reading** performance;

• offer opportunities for **repeated readings** of progressively more difficult texts;

• support prosody development by **chunking phrases** and by interspersing formal readings with short humorous passages.

Have students form partners and listen to one another read. After students have seen the teacher guide students in reading with expression, the students can help each other to practice reading with these fluency skills.

Called by some educators as a "gateway" skill, fluency is important for all students. Through it, they are able to access the knowledge and skills that they need to fully acquire the skills needed to become good readers.

The Cremation of Sam McGee

by Robert Service

There are strange things done in the midnight sun
    By the men who moil for gold;
The Arctic trails have their secret tales
    That would make your blood run cold;
The Northern Lights have seen queer sights,
    But the queerest they ever did see
Was that night on the marge, of Lake Lebarge
    I cremated Sam McGee.

Now Sam McGee was from Tennessee,
    where the cotton blooms and blows.
Why he left his home in the South to roam
    'round the Pole, God only knows.
He was always cold, but the land of gold
    seemed to hold him like a spell;
Though he'd often say in his homely way
    that "he'd sooner live in hell."

On a Christmas Day we were mushing our way
    over the Dawson trail.
Talk of your cold! through the parka's fold
    it stabbed like a driven nail.
If our eyes we'd close, then the lashes froze
    till sometimes we couldn't see;
It wasn't much fun, but the only one
    to whimper was Sam McGee.

And that very night, as we lay packed tight
    in our robes beneath the snow,
And the dogs were fed, and the stars o'erhead
    were dancing heel and toe,
He turned to me, and "Cap," says he,
    "I'll cash in this trip, I guess;
And if I do, I'm asking that you
    won't refuse my last request."

Well, he seemed so low that I couldn't say no;
    then he says with a sort of moan:
"It's the cursed cold, and it's got right hold
    till I'm chilled clean through to the bone.
Yet 'tain't being dead—it's my awful dread
    of the icy grave that pains;
So I want you to swear that, foul or fair,
    you'll cremate my last remains."

A pal's last need is a thing to heed,
    so I swore I would not fail;
And we started on at the streak of dawn;
    but God! he looked ghastly pale.
He crouched on the sleigh, and he raved all day
    of his home in Tennessee;
And before nightfall a corpse was all
    that was left of Sam McGee.

There wasn't a breath in that land of death,
    and I hurried, horror driven,
With a corpse half hid that I couldn't get rid,
    because of a promise given;
It was lashed to the sleigh, and it seemed to say:
    "You may tax your brawn and brains,
But you promised true, and it's up to you
    to cremate those last remains."

Now a promise made is a debt unpaid,
    and the trail has its own stern code.
In the days to come, though my lips were dumb,
    in my heart how I cursed that load.
In the long, long night, by the lone firelight,
    while the huskies, round in a ring,
Howled out their woes to the homeless snows—
    O God! how I loathed the thing.

And every day that quiet clay
    seemed to heavy and heavier grow;
And on I went, though the dogs were spent
    and the grub was getting low;
The trail was bad, and I felt half mad,
    but I swore I would not give in;
And I'd often sing to the hateful thing,
    and it hearkened with a grin.

Till I came to the marge of Lake Lebarge,
    and a derelict there lay;
It was jammed in the ice, but I saw in a trice
    it was called the "Alice May."
And I looked at it, and I thought a bit,
    and I looked at my frozen chum;
Then "Here," said I, with a sudden cry,
    "is my cre-ma-tor-eum."

Some planks I tore from the cabin floor,
    and I lit the boiler fire;
Some coal I found that was lying around,
    and I heaped the fuel higher;
The flames just soared, and the furnace roared—
    such a blaze you seldom see;
And I burrowed a hole in the glowing coal,
    and I stuffed in Sam McGee.

Then I made a hike, for I didn't like
    to hear him sizzle so;
And the heavens scowled, and the huskies howled,
    and the wind began to blow.
It was icy cold, but the hot sweat rolled
    down my cheeks, and I don't know why;
And the greasy smoke in an inky cloak
    went streaking down the sky.

I do not know how long in the snow
    I wrestled with grisly fear;
But the stars came out and they danced about
    Ere again I ventured near;
I was sick with dread, but I bravely said:
    "I'll just take a peep inside.
I guess he's cooked, and it's time I looked,"
    . . . then the door I opened wide.

And there sat Sam, looking cool and calm,
    in the heart of the furnace roar;
And he wore a smile you could see a mile,
    and he said: "Please close that door.
It's fine in here, but I greatly fear
    you'll let in the cold and storm—
Since I left Plumtree, down in Tennessee,
    it's the first time I've been warm."

There are strange things done in the midnight sun
    By the men who moil for gold;
The Arctic trails have their secret tales
    That would make your blood run cold;
The Northern Lights have seen queer sights,
    But the queerest they ever did see
Was that night on the marge of Lake Lebarge
    I cremated Sam McGee.

from **The Monsters Are Due on Maple Street**

by Rod Serling

NARRATOR'S VOICE. Maple Street. Six-forty-four P.M. on a late September evening, [A pause.] Maple Street in the last calm and reflective moment . . . before the monsters came!

[The camera slowly pans across the porches again. We see a man screwing a light bulb on a front porch, then getting down off the stool to flick the switch and finding that nothing happens. Another man is working on an electric power mower. He plugs in the plug, flicks on the switch of the power mower, off and on, with nothing happening. Through the window of a front porch, we see a woman pushing her finger back and forth on the dial hook. Her voice is indistinct and distant, but intelligible and repetitive.]

WOMAN. Operator, operator, something's wrong on the phone, operator!

[MRS. BRAND comes out on the porch and calls to STEVE.]

MRS. BRAND. [Calling.] Steve, the power's off. I had the soup on the stove and the stove just stopped working.

WOMAN. Same thing over here. I can't get anybody on the phone either. The phone seems to be dead.

[We look down on the street as we hear the voices creep up from below, small, mildly disturbed voices highlighting these kinds of phrases:]

VOICES.

Electricity's off.

Phone won't work.

Can't get a thing on the radio.

My power mower won't move, won't work at all.

Radio's gone dead!

[PETE VAN HORN, a tall, thin man, is seen standing in front of his house.]

VAN HORN. I'll cut through the backyard . . . See if the power's still on on Floral Street. I'll be right back!

[He walks past the side of his house and disappears into the backyard. The camera pans down slowly until we're looking at ten or eleven people standing around the street and overflowing to the curb and sidewalk. In the background is STEVE BRAND's car.]

STEVE. Doesn't make sense. Why should the power go off all of a sudden, and the phone line?

DON. Maybe some sort of an electrical storm or something.

CHARLIE. That don't seem likely. Sky's just as blue as anything. Not a cloud. No lightning. No thunder. No nothing. How could it be a storm?

WOMAN. I can't get a thing on the radio. Not even the portable.

[The people again murmur softly in wonderment and question.]

CHARLIE. Well, why don't you go downtown and check with the police, though they'll probably think we're crazy or something. A little power failure and right away we get all flustered and everything.

STEVE. It isn't just the power failure, Charlie. If it was, we'd still be able to get a broadcast on the portable.

[There's a murmur of reaction to this. STEVE looks from face to face and then over to his car.]

STEVE. I'll run downtown. We'll get this all straightened out.

[He walks over to the car, gets in it, turns the key. Looking through the open car door, we see the crowd watching him from the other side. STEVE starts the engine. It turns over sluggishly and then just stops dead. He tries it again and this time he can't get it to turn over. Then, very slowly and reflectively, he turns the key back to "off" and slowly gets out of the car. The people stare at STEVE. He stands for a moment by the car, then walks toward the group.]

STEVE. I don't understand it. It was working fine before . . .

DON. Out of gas?

STEVE. [Shakes his head.] I just had it filled up.

WOMAN. What's it mean?

CHARLIE. It's just as if . . . as if everything had stopped. [Then he turns toward STEVE.] We'd better walk downtown. [Another murmur of assent at this.]

STEVE. The two of us can go, Charlie. [He turns to look back at the car.] It couldn't be the meteor. A meteor couldn't do this.

[He and CHARLIE exchange a look, then they start to walk away from the group. We see TOMMY, a serious-faced fourteen-year-old in spectacles who stands a few feet away from the group. He is halfway between them and the two men, who start to walk down the sidewalk.]

TOMMY. Mr. Brand . . . you better not!

STEVE. Why not?

TOMMY. They don't want you to.

[STEVE and CHARLIE exchange a grin, and STEVE looks back toward the boy.]

STEVE. Who doesn't want us to?

TOMMY. [Jerks his head in the general direction of the distant horizon.] Them!

STEVE. Them?

CHARLIE. Who are them?

TOMMY. [Very intently.] Whoever was in that thing that came by overhead.

[STEVE knits his brows for a moment, cocking his head questioningly. His voice is intense.]

STEVE. What?

TOMMY. Whoever was in that thing that came over. I don't think they want us to leave here.

[STEVE leaves CHARLIE and walks over to the boy. He kneels down in front of him. He forces his voice to remain gentle. He reaches out and holds the boy.]

STEVE. What do you mean? What are you talking about?

TOMMY. They don't want us to leave. That's why they shut everything off.

STEVE. What makes you say that? Whatever gave you that idea?

WOMAN. [From the crowd.] Now isn't that the craziest thing you ever heard?

TOMMY. [Persistently but a little intimidated by the crowd.] It's always that way, in every story I ever read about a ship landing from outer space.

WOMAN. [To the boy's mother, SALLY, who stands on the fringe of the crowd.] From outer space, yet! Sally, you better get that boy of yours up to bed. He's been reading too many comic books or seeing too many movies or something.

from **I Have a Dream**

by Martin Luther King Jr.

It is obvious today that America has defaulted on this promissory note in so far as her citizens of color are concerned. Instead of honoring the sacred obligation, America has given the Negro people a bad check, a check which has come back marked "insufficient funds." We refuse to believe that there are insufficient funds in the great vaults of opportunity of this nation. And so we've come to cash this check, a check that will give us upon demand the riches of freedom and the security of justice.

We have also come to this hallowed spot to remind America of the fierce urgency of now. This is no time to engage in the luxury of cooling off or take the tranquilizing drug of gradualism. Now is the time to make real the promises of democracy; now is the time to rise from the dark and desolate valley of segregation to the sunlit path of racial justice; now is the time to lift our nation from the quicksands of racial injustice to the solid rock of brotherhood; now is the time to make justice a reality for all God's children.

from **A Child's Christmas in Wales**

by Dylan Thomas

It was on the afternoon of the day of Christmas Eve, and I was in Mrs. Prothero's garden, waiting for cats, with her son Jim. It was snowing. It was always snowing at Christmas. December, in my memory, is white as Lapland, though there were no reindeers. But there were cats. Patient, cold, and callous, our hands wrapped in socks, we waited to snowball the cats. Sleek and long as jaguars and horrible-whiskered, spitting and snarling, they would slink and sidle over the white back-garden walls, and the lynx-eyed hunters, Jim and I, fur-capped and moccasined trappers from Hudson Bay, off Mumbles Road, would hurl our deadly snowballs at the green of their eyes.

The wise cats never appeared. We were so still, Eskimo-footed arctic marksmen in the muffling silence of the eternal snows—eternal, ever since Wednesday—that we never heard Mrs. Prothero's first cry from her igloo at the bottom of the garden. Or, if we heard it at all, it was, to us, like the far-off challenge of our enemy and prey, the neighbour's polar cat. But soon the voice grew louder. "Fire!" cried Mrs. Prothero, and she beat the dinner-gong.

And we ran down the garden, with the snowballs in our arms, toward the house; and smoke, indeed, was pouring out of the dining-room, and the gong was bombilating, and Mrs. Prothero was announcing ruin like a town crier in Pompeii. This was better than all the cats in Wales standing on the wall in a row. We bounded into the house, laden with snow-balls, and stopped at the open door of the smoke-filled room.

Something was burning all right; perhaps it was Mr. Prothero, who always slept there after midday dinner with a newspaper over his face. But he was standing in the middle of the room, saying, "A fine Christmas!" and smacking at the smoke with a slipper. "Call the fire brigade," cried Mrs. Prothero as she beat the gong.

"They won't be there," said Mr. Prothero, "it's Christmas."

There was no fire to be seen, only clouds of smoke and Mr. Prothero standing in the middle of them, waving his slipper as though he were conducting.

"Do something," he said.

And we threw all our snowballs into the smoke—I think we missed Mr. Prothero—and ran out of the house to the telephone box.

"Let's call the police as well," Jim said.

"And the ambulance."

"And Ernie Jenkins, he likes fires."